Magic In Minutes

(Easy to do magic tricks and party planning secrets all in one book!)

- **Turn Water Into Ice**
- **Read Minds**
- **Perform Psychic Feats**
- **Perform Amazing Card Tricks**
- **Twist Your Arms In An Impossible Manner**
- **Float Yourself Off The Ground**

Bonus: Party Planning Guide Included Free!!!

by Ed Junior

ISBN: 1-4107-1816-6 (e-book)
ISBN: 1-4107-1817-4 (Paperback)

Library of Congress Control Number: 2003090638

This book is printed on acid free paper.

Printed in the United States of America
Bloomington, IN

1stBooks – rev. 03/12/03

Photo Courtesy of Primrose Studios, Don Chaffe

<u>This book is dedicated to my entire family for continued support in</u>

<u>my full time career as a professional entertainer.</u>

TABLE OF CONTENTS

INTRODUCTION

There are so many great books on magic. Every time I visit my local bookstore I always search for magic books that I might not have in my collection. I felt it was time for me to compile my favorite tricks and put them all in one book. In this book you will find many of the greatest, but simple magic tricks that you will be able to perform almost anywhere at anytime. This type of magic is known as impromptu. To my knowledge there is no one source for impromptu magic tricks. Most of the magic tricks do not require any advanced setup or preparation. I have added a few tricks that will require preparation. I have done this so you will get the most information and become knowledgeable about the different types of magic that exists. All of these tricks were and still are used by some of today's most famous magicians. You will find a wide variety of impromptu tricks ranging from money, cards, and mind reading tricks. Most of the items used can be found in any home, office, or restaurant. I urge you to read through and mark down which magic tricks catch your interest. Please be sure to practice them before presenting them to anyone. Children to adults will find magic tricks they can perform.

Rules of Magic:

Before we begin with the magic please be sure to read and abide by the magic rules. This is the key to successful magic.

1. **Practice** the magic trick

2. **Practice** the magic trick again

3. **Practice** the magic trick again (Practice Makes You Good)

4. Never repeat a magic trick

5. Never tell or giveaway the secret

These rules are simple to follow. Please practice the trick before performing it for a stranger. If you don't practice enough you could mess up and ruin it for the spectators. After you feel comfortable with a trick perform it for a friend or family member. They will be a good audience to test your magic tricks on. Ask them for some feedback so you can decide if you should practice more or change your patter. Lastly, never expose a magic secret. When you expose a magic secret it looses its impact on the audience you performed for. Keep the tricks to yourself and have fun!

Magic Terms:

Here is a list of some magic terms magicians often use to describe their methods and routines.

- Patter (a story line, or words spoken during the magic trick)

- Routine (many magic tricks all flowing together)

- Forcing (making the spectator choose an item or card you want them too)

- Palming (secretly holding an object in your hand)

- Reset (setting up the magic trick again for performance)

- Misdirection (misdirecting the audiences attention to secretly accomplish a magic trick)

- Method (the secret to a magic trick)

- <u>Illusion</u> (a large magic trick usually involving a person or persons)

- <u>Spectator</u> (a person who is watching you perform)

- <u>Impromptu</u> (being able to perform magic at anytime and anywhere)

- <u>Prediction</u> (fortune telling, an accurate guess to future events)

- <u>Sleight of Hand</u> (magic using pure skill, manipulating objects in the hands)

- <u>Flourish</u> (a dramatic show of skill, often used in magic routines to add texture)

- <u>Gimmick</u> (a hidden device used to create a magic trick)

- <u>Effect</u> (a word to describe what the spectators believe they see)

- <u>Dealing</u> (when cards are taken off the deck and placed on the table)

- <u>Shuffling</u> (a term used when mixing the cards, changing their order)

Here is a brief list of magic words you can use when you are performing your favorite magic trick!

- Hocus Pocus

- Abracadabra

- Flim Flam

- Presto

- It's Magic

Now, time for some magic! You will note each trick has a scale of difficulty: easy, medium and difficult. I have also added a scale of impressiveness. The scale is 1-10. 10 will represent the most impressive and 1 will represent the least impressive. This will tell you how exciting the trick is to the audience when you perform it.

Creating A Style

In magic it is very important that you create some sort of character or style. Theses two traits make magicians unique. Magic would be boring if every magician talked the same way, wore the same clothes, performed the same type of magic and so on. Just look at David Copperfield. His style is modern and dramatic. He wears modern clothes and uses modern music. If I compared David Copperfield to David Blaine I could list many differences. Here are some examples:

1. David Copperfield performs mostly stage magic; David Blaine performs mostly close-up or street magic.

2. David Blaine is more mysterious and to the point, David Copperfield is more oriented

in telling a story with his illusions and he adds comedy to his show.

Can you think of any more differences? To get the most out of the magic you learn you need to create a style and character as I said before. This will separate you from the rest of the pack. Be different. Try and think of ways you could add aspects of your everyday life to your magic. Do you want to be mysterious, comical or dramatic? Take your time when developing a style. The more time you dedicate to practicing the easier it will be for you to find your performing style or character. Have fun creating, and be different!

Impromptu
Card Feats

Ed Junior

Impromptu Card Tricks

Magicians are famous for being able to take an ordinary deck of cards and perform miracles with it. This section will cover card trick basics. These card tricks are easy to do but very impressive to an audience. I suggest using Bicycle brand playing cards. It is important to practice these tricks thoroughly so you can build up your confidence in handling the cards. Never perform with a brand new deck because the cards are extremely slippery right out of the box. If you have a new deck shuffle them numerous times and break them in by bending the deck back and forth. Do not crease the cards though. Breaking in the deck will allow you to handle it much easier. Don't forget to discard the advertising cards before performing.

It is not necessary to perform all of the card tricks in this section. Pick one or two that you like and learn them. When you are going to a party or having friends over always try and carry a deck of cards in your pocket. This will give you the chance to perform some card tricks impromptu.

Fantastic Ace

Effect:

The magician displays three of the aces to a spectator and names them out loud one by one. The magician snaps his fingers and squares the cards up. The aces are once again displayed but the ace of diamonds has changed into the ace of hearts. The magician produces the ace of diamonds from his pocket.

Difficulty: medium

Impressiveness: 6

Method:

You only need the four aces for this trick. Place the ace of diamonds in your pocket. You now have to setup the cards so it looks like your holding the ace of clubs, ace of diamonds and the ace of spades. Place the ace of hearts in the middle of the black aces. You are actually putting it under the other two. Line up the cards so the heart is covered up so it resembles a diamond. You are ready to begin. Show the two black aces and the ace of diamonds in the middle. You may name the cards out loud, be sure you name the ace of diamonds in the middle. Square up the cards. Snap your fingers and say a magic word. Lay the cards on the table showing that the ace of diamonds has changed into the ace of hearts. Tell the spectators that it didn't fly to far, just to your pocket. Pull out the ace of

diamonds from your pocket and lay it next to the others.

Suggestions:

This is a great trick that requires a little setup. Make sure

the cards are lined up perfectly before performing it.

(Fantastic Ace Setup)

Fantastic Five

Effect:

A card is selected and lost in the deck. One card is discovered face up in the deck, but it is not the selected card, it is a five. You count down five cards to find the selected card. The other four counted cards are aces.

Difficulty: easy

Impressiveness: 7

Method:

From the bottom of the deck: place the four aces, any five face up, and the remainder of the deck. Now you are setup and ready to perform the trick.

Have a card selected and returned to the top of the deck. Cut the deck, bringing the stack of cards onto the selection. Spread the deck revealing the five. Next count down five

7

cards and reveal the selected card. Finally, reveal that the four cards between the five and the selected card are the aces!

Suggestions:

When the spectator selects a card make sure you don't spread the cards to far revealing the upside down five.

Easy Card Force:

Utility:

This is not a magic trick. This is a magic utility move that can be applied to many tricks. The easy card force is used to make the spectator select a particular card. It is very versatile and deceptive.

Difficulty: medium

Impressiveness:

Method:

You need a regular deck of cards. Lets assume that you want to force the ace of hearts on a spectator. To do this you need to setup the deck. Before you begin any trick place your force card (in this case, ace of hearts) on the top of the deck. To perform this force, take the cards out of the box. Ask a spectator to cut the cards in half and to place that half aside of the remaining half. Have him flip the half he cut upside down and replace it back on the other half. Ask him to cut deeper than last time and to place this portion aside. Have him flip this portion upside down and replace on the rest of the deck. Ask him to discard the cards that are face up. When the spectator arrives at the first face down card have him look at it and memorize it. The card he memorizes is your original force card the ace of hearts.

Suggestions:

Remember any card that you want to force needs to be placed on top of the deck before your perform. Setup the deck when no one is looking. Even though cutting the deck seems so random and haphazard the first face down card will always be your force card. When the spectator arrives at the face down card, remind him that he cut the deck at random and flipped the deck in all directions. Also tell him that the first face down card is the card <u>he</u> cut too. This easy card force will allow you to literally do dozens of tricks. Lets look at some magic tricks using this easy card force.

Card Pulse

Effect:

The spectator cuts to a card and memorizes it. The spectator then is asked to shuffle the cards and to spread the cards out on the table so every card is visible. The magician claims he can locate the selected card by feeling the spectators pulse. The magician feels the spectators pulse and successfully finds the selected card.

Difficulty: medium

Impressiveness: 8

Method:

Choose a force card and place it on top of the deck. Lets assume it is the ace of hearts. Perform the easy card force. After the spectator memorizes his card instruct him to place the card back in the deck and shuffle. Have him now spread the cards face up on the table so every card is visible. Tell the spectator you will locate his card by feeling his pulse. Grab his wrist pretending to feel for his pulse. Move his hand over top the cards. As you come across the ace of hearts announce that his pulse seems to be beating faster. Pick up the ace of hearts and take your well-deserved applause.

Suggestions:

This is a favorite trick of mine. It is very easy to do and carries a big impact. Take your time when trying to locate their card. Really try and feel their pulse. This will add excitement to the trick.

The Amazing Four Of A Kind

Effect:

The spectator cuts to a card and flips it face up so everyone can see. The magician takes three cards from his pocket and places them face down next to the selection. The cards are turned face up revealing the three mates matching the selected card.

Difficulty: medium

Impressiveness: 8

Method:

Before you begin choose any four of a kind. For example: all the kings. Take three of the kings and place in your pocket. Place the remaining king on top of the deck. You are now ready to begin. Perform the easy card force. Have the spectator flip his selected card face up. Pull out the three cards from your pocket and place them face down next to the selection. Have the spectator flip the cards from you pocket face up. You have three kings and the spectator completes the four of a kind with the last card.

Suggestions:

You can also tell the spectator that you have prediction cards in your pocket. This makes the trick more of a mind reading stunt than a trick.

Fantastic Prediction

Effect:

The magician places an envelope on the table containing a prediction. The spectator cuts to a card and memorizes it. The prediction envelope is opened and the prediction is announced. The prediction matches the selected card.

Difficulty: easy

Impressiveness: 9

Method:

Place your force card on top of the deck. Write the cards name on a piece of paper and seal it in an envelope. Place your prediction on the table and announce that you will see into the future. Perform the easy card force. Have the spectator memorize the card. Have him open the prediction and announce it to everyone. Accept your applause.

Suggestions:

Before you are asked to perform, it is a good idea to have your force card on top of the deck and your prediction sealed in an envelope. Never setup a trick while your audience is around.

Card Cheat

Effect:

The magician claims that the spectator is a card cheat. The spectator cuts to four cards and lays them on the table aside of each other. The cards are revealed and shown to be the four aces.

Difficulty: medium

Impressiveness: 7

Method:

Take any four of a kind and place them on top of the deck. I prefer the aces. Perform the easy card force but have them remove the first four face down cards. In the regular easy card force only one is removed. Have him place the four cards on the table keeping them face down. Tell the spectator that you believe he is a card cheat. Reveal the four face down cards to be all four aces! The spectator does all the work for this miracle.

Suggestion:

Try and create some patter for this magic trick. A good idea is to explain how people cheat at playing cards. Tell him that he looks like he would be a cheater. The spectator will look at you like your crazy. When the four aces are revealed he is in disbelief. You can also use a different four of a kind.

Ed Junior

Impromptu Mind Reading Feats

Ed Junior

Impromptu Mind Reading Feats

This section covers mind reading feats that are easy and fun to perform. Mind reading has been around for thousands of years. Fortunetellers and tarot card readers are more common names for mind readers. The people who claim they are able to read peoples minds or have control over what people think and do always fascinate the public. There has been a huge growth of psychics and psychic services in this country such as television shows, seminars, psychic phone services, etc. There are many props used in mind reading today such as; tarot cards, crystal balls and pendulums. The feats in this section use simple items such as a pad of paper and pencil or dice. If you use these feats at the proper time people will start giving you credit for having amazing psychic powers!

<u>Mystic Crayons</u>

Effect:

You hand a box of crayons to the spectator. Asking them to pick out one crayon and place it in your hands behind your back so you cannot see a thing. The crayon is taken back and placed in the box. The magician then asks the spectator to concentrate on the color crayon they chose. The magician correctly names the color of the chosen crayon!

Difficulty: Easy

Impressiveness: 9

Method:

Even though your back is turned and there is no way for you to see the crayon you secretly scrape or smear the crayon on your fingernail. When the spectator is placing the crayon back in the box this is your chance to bring your hands around and secretly glimpse at your fingernail. You should clearly see what color crayon was chosen.

Suggestions:

Make sure the spectator has all the crayons in the box before you announce the color chosen. Take your time, and build up the suspense. Make them concentrate really hard and have them mentally send the image to you. I would

Ed Junior

suggest using a small 8-color box of crayons. Stick with the

primary color crayons.

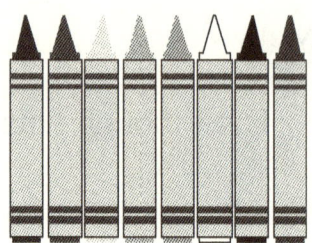

Secretly scrape the crayon on your thumbnail.

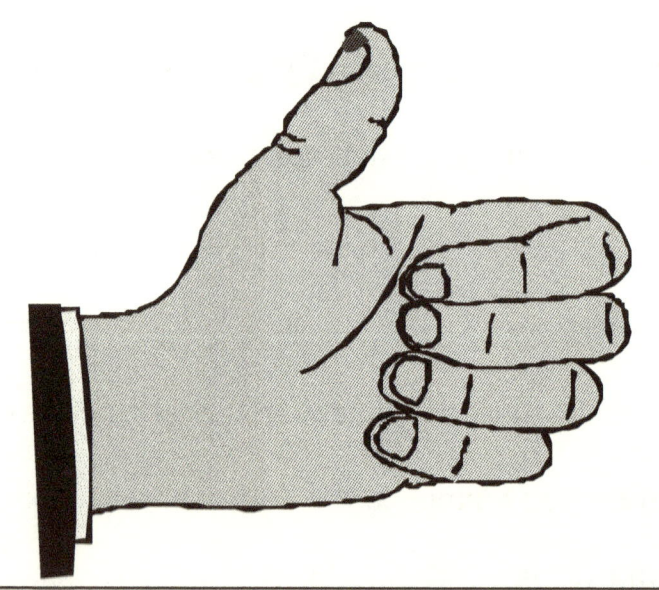

The Math Magician

Effect:

The magician shows a sealed envelope containing a prediction. It is placed on the table. A spectator is asked to write down a 3-digit number making sure the first digit is higher than the other two. The spectator is now asked to reverse these numbers and to subtract them from the first set of numbers. Next the spectator is asked to take each individual digit and add them all together. The total is announced loudly so everyone can hear it. The spectator opens the prediction and it matches their total!

Difficulty: easy

Impressiveness: 6

Method:

This is a great magic trick based on mathematics. Write down the number 18 on a piece of paper and seal it in an envelope. The number 18 will be the answer every single time if the instructions are followed correctly. Have them follow the steps all the way through. First have them write down any three digit number making sure to tell them that the first digit needs to be higher than the other two. Example: 652. Have them reverse the digits. Example: 256. Have them subtract the numbers. 652-256=396. Finally, have them add up each digit individually. Example: 3+9+6=18. Tell them to concentrate on the total they have arrived at. Have them tear open the envelope and read your prediction out loud. 18!

Suggestions:

Carry a few small envelopes with you in your pocket containing your prediction of 18. Then you will be ready to perform the effect on a moments notice. The only other things you need are a spectator, a pencil and a piece of paper. Don't do this trick more than once for the same person because the answer always comes to 18.

The Magic of 1089

Effect:

Magician has the spectator do a few calculations to arrive at a seemingly random number. A prediction envelope is opened and it matches the spectators number.

Difficulty: medium

Impressiveness: 8

Method:

This is similar to the other mathematical trick. The result of this calculation will always be 1089. This is a bit more deceptive because there are a few extra calculations. Here is the formula you should memorize. Follow it exactly. Ask the spectator to pick a three-digit number and write it down on a piece of paper, making sure all the digits are different. Have them reverse the number and write it directly below. Instruct them to subtract the smaller number from the larger number. Now ask them if they have a two-digit number or a three-digit number. If they say that they have a two-digit number tell them to write a zero in front of those two digits. Proceed if they have a three-digit number. Now reverse those three digits and write them directly below your last set of numbers. Add the last two sets of numbers together. The answer will always be 1089.

Formula Example: <u>842-248= 594+495=1089</u> or <u>918-819=099+990=1089</u>

Suggestions:

Don't perform both of these mathematical tricks at the same time. Do one of them and save the other for a different time.

Easy Dice It

Effect:

A spectator is asked to roll a pair of dice, stack them on top of one another, and add up the sides of the dice that do not show. The magician announces the total the spectator has without even looking at them.

Difficulty: medium

Impressiveness: 7

Method:

Hand a pair of dice to a spectator and have him roll them. Instruct him to roll the dice and to make sure each dice has a different number on it. Give these instructions while your back is turned to the spectator. Ask the spectator to roll the dice again and to place one of them on top of the other in a stack. Turn around to look if they have done this properly. If so, turn back around. Write down a prediction on a piece of paper. Ask the spectator to add the numbers of the dice that are not showing. Example: The side that is facing down on the table, and the two sides of the dice that are touching each other. The number you predict will match the numbers the spectator has added up. To do this: When you turn around to make sure the dice are stacked properly you secretly glimpse the top of the die. In your mind subtract this number from 14. This number will give you the total of the three sides of the dice that are not showing. After you know the number this will be the prediction that you need to write down. This works because the opposites sides of every dice add up to 7. You are using two dice so it will be 14.

Suggestions:

Practice this one. It's fun, amazing, and packs small!

Add the number of the die that is face down on the table to the other numbers that are touching each other. See arrows.

Simple Mind

Effect:

A spectator is asked to think of a small number between 1-10. Some easy calculations are performed and the magician is able to predict the spectators number correctly.

Difficulty: easy

Impressiveness: 6

Method:

This effect is simple. You need to remember the following formula. Ask a spectator to think of a number between 1-10. Now have them double that number. Now ask them to add 8 to it. Next divide that number by two. Finally, subtract your original number that you chose. This works because the spectator was asked to add 8. The answer will always be 4. You can write your prediction down on a piece of paper. Put your prediction in an envelope and seal it. Write, PREDICTION on the envelope. This will catch the attention of everyone. After the spectator has a number have him open your prediction and read it to everyone.

Suggestions:

Make sure the spectator has a pencil and paper to work out the calculations. This makes it much easier.

Ed Junior

Impromptu
Psychic Feats

Impromptu Psychic Feats

This section is very similar to mind reading feats. However in this section all of the tests and experiments deal more with mind over matter. Here you will display your mental power upon spectators rather than just reading their minds. These tests are great in conjunction with any of the mind reading feats in the earlier section. See which ones work the best for you. After you are comfortable with these tests I suggest that you work on your presentation and character style. This will make everything much more believable and it will add texture to your act.

Do real Psychics exist?

The fact is all of the so-called "psychics" are actually entertainers using magic techniques. The general public accepts these people as genuine psychics because they are not billed as a magician or illusionist. "Psychics" such as John Edwards and Sylvia Brown are good examples of entertainers who use magic techniques. Of course none of them will ever admit it. The reason I explain this is so you get a good understanding of what magic is all about. Magic covers a wide range of topics and is not limited only to card tricks or the famous magic wand. This book should give you a good idea on what magic has to offer. Now its time for some Psychic Feats!

No Pulse

Effect:

Magician announces that it is possible to stop his pulse. To display this feat of psychic powers he asks a spectator to grab his wrist and find his pulse. The spectator feels his pulse beating. The pulse seemingly disappears slowly, little by little until a pulse is no longer detected.

Difficulty: medium

Impressiveness: 9

Method:

To accomplish the feat of psychic powers you need a small rubber ball or handkerchief tied in a hard bulky knot. Which ever you choose place it underneath of your arm. To slow down your pulse simply apply pressure with your arm against the ball or handkerchief.

Suggestions:

This trick is easy to accomplish if you are wearing a coat or jacket. The sleeves will cover your arm thereby hiding the secret. Find an opportune time to place the ball under your arm. Make sure the spectator can find your pulse beating before applying pressure. They will think you have psychic powers!

Place ball or handkerchief here.

The Pocket Psychic

Effect:

You pull a small pendulum out of your pocket. On a piece of paper you make a large circle. Hand the pendulum to a spectator and ask them to hold it over the paper but to keep their arm still as much as possible. You ask the Pocket Psychic numerous "yes" and "no" questions. A "yes" answer will swing the pendulum back and forth. A "no" answer will swing it in circles.

Method:

No one really knows why this happens. Many feel it works on unnoticed muscle glitches in the arm and hand.

Suggestions:

Make the pendulum out of string and a simple penny tied to the bottom. You may use a small crystal on a necklace also. In this trick the piece of paper with the circle on it is merely a prop. It is not necessarily needed. Use your imagination but keep in mind that you need a bit of weight at the end of the string. Have the spectator ask the Pocket Psychic questions. Have fun with this one. It packs in your pocket and can be performed anytime!

Magnetic Chair

Effect:

The magician claims that he can make any chair magnetized. One who sits in the chair will not be able to get up. A spectator sits in the chair with his feet on the ground, back against the chair, and tilting his head backwards. The magician places one finger on the spectators head to increase the magnetic field. The spectator tries to move and get up but he does not succeed. The magnetic fields slowly decrease and the magician removes his finger. The spectator finds it very easy to get out of the chair.

Difficulty: easy

Impressiveness: 8

Method:

Make sure the spectator in the chair has his feet on the ground, back against the chair, arms folded on his lap, and his head tilted back. Simply place your index finger on his forehead and ask the spectator to try and get up. He will not be able to because his center of gravity is unbalanced. His center of gravity is too far back. Make sure you position and instruct the spectator properly to achieve this trick.

Suggestions:

Practice with a friend. If you do not succeed at first ask the spectator to extend his legs outward. This might make it easier to do but it is not as deceptive.

Head Games

Effect:

The magician announces he can weaken the strength of a volunteer without them realizing it. He places his hand on top of his head and instructs the spectator to move it from its position. The spectator uses all of his strength but does not succeed.

Difficulty: easy

Impressiveness: 9

Method:

To make this work just apply pressure with your hand against the top of your head. The pressure is so strong that no one will be able to lift your hand off of your head.

Suggestions:

When you first show this stunt to someone do not apply pressure at all. The spectator will easily lift your hand off. Then tell him that you can weaken him. Play this up a little and build suspense. Wave your hands at him in all kinds of magical gestures; say magic words, anything you can think of. Then repeat the stunt and apply pressure. The spectator will not be able to lift your hand.

In Control

Effect:

The magician puts a hypnotic spell on a spectator. The spectator closes his eyes and follows a few easy instructions. The spectator when instructed is to try and open their eyes. The spectator is unable to do so until the hypnotic spell is stopped.

Difficulty: medium

Impressiveness: 7

Method:

You must instruct the spectator to follow your directions. Tell him to look up without moving his head. Tell him to concentrate on looking up for a few seconds. Ask him to close his eyelids while continuing to look up. He must keep his eyes in the same position when they are

closed. Pretend to cast a hypnotic spell on him by holding your hand on his head. Now instruct him that since you set a spell on him he will be unable to open his eyelids. He will fail in his attempt. Tell him to relax and that you will take the spell away. He can now open his eyes. This magic stunt works by using the muscles in the eyes. When your eyes are looking up and your eyes are closed it is very difficult to open your eyelids. Try it, and have fun.

Suggestions:

Learn a few of these mental feats and you will soon have a nice routine that you can perform almost anywhere. When performing any of these feats do not tell your audience that you are doing a trick. This takes the entertainment value out of your performance. Refer to these mental feats as hypnotic experiments or psychic powers.

Strong or Weak

Effect:

A spectator is asked to try and separate your fingers that you have touched together. He is unable to do so because you seem to have psychic powers.

Difficulty: easy

Impressiveness: 8

Method:

This mental feat works because you are exerting more energy and power then the spectator will be able too. Hold you arms at chest level and touch your index finger of each hand together. Instruct the spectator to grab both of your wrists and to try and pull your fingers apart. They will not be able too. The position of your arms and hands is key for this mental feat to work. They will be unable to exert enough power to separate your fingers.

Suggestions:

Try this on everyone. Start with someone who is your size and then try it on someone who is bigger than you. It is a very impressive stunt.

Impromptu Séance

Effect:

The magician tells the spectator that it is possible to contact the dead at anytime and anywhere. Instruct the spectator too close their eyes as you place both index fingers over them. The dead are instructed to show themselves in any means possible. The spectator feels something touch them on the shoulder. Your fingers are removed and the eyes of the spectator are open. The room is empty except for you and the spectator.

Difficulty: medium

Impressiveness: 9

Method:

This mental feat can only be performed for one person at a time and should only be done when no one else is watching. Hold each of your hands up with your index fingers extended. Hold your fingers at the spectators eye level. Instruct them to shut their eyes. As they do this drop your left hand to the side and extend your index and middle finger of your right hand. Place these fingers over the spectators eyelids. The spectator believes both fingers of each hand are touching their eyes. Tap the spectator lightly on their shoulder and immediately ask the spectator to open their eyes. As soon as you do this bring up both hands and extend your index fingers as before. Draw your hands in. The spectator will have felt something touch them.

Suggestion:

Instead of touching the spectator have a rattle or noisemaker near by. Use your free hand to make the noise.

Think of other ways and objects with which you can perform this miracle.

As soon as their eyes are closed, place your pointer and middle finger of one hand over their eyelids.

Making Magic
At Home

Making Magic At Home

This section covers magic tricks that need to be built using items that can be found in your home. I hope to give you a good idea on how you can take ordinary items and make them magical. Since these tricks require you to build a prop you need to make sure your audience does not handle the prop at all. If they pickup your props and give it a close look they might see the secret to how a trick works. These tricks are good to perform standing up with a good-sized crowd watching.

Here is a brief list of supplies you will need.

1. Scissors

2. Glue

3. Old Playing Cards

4. Tape

5. Sponge

6. Opaque Cup

Fantastic Rising Card

Effect:

A card is selected and placed on top of the deck. The deck is placed in the card box. The flap mysteriously opens by itself and out rises the selected card!

Difficulty: medium

Impressiveness: 8

Method:

Prepare a card box by cutting a small opening in the back. The opening should be large enough for your index finger to fit. The section that gets cut out should be the middle of the card box near the top. Once the cut out is complete place the entire deck back inside. To perform the trick take out the cards and have a spectator select one. Place the selected card back on top of the deck. Tell your audience that you will isolate the deck by placing it in the box. Grip the box in your prominent hand and secretly use your index finger to slowly push up on the selected card. It will push open the flap and will mysteriously rise from the card box!

Suggestion:

Make sure the spectator does not see the cut out in the card box at anytime. After the card is selected make sure you place the deck in the box so that the selected card is against the cut out. You should practice making the card rise slowly and smoothly. Be sure to keep your hand still as much as possible.

The Balancing Cup

Effect:

The magician places a cup full of liquid carefully on top of a playing card. He removes his hands and the cup seems to be balancing on the edge of the playing card.

Difficulty: medium

Impressiveness: 7

Method:

For this trick you need to construct a gimmick. Cut a playing card in half-length wise. Attach this piece to the back of another card using a piece of strong clear tape. This piece will act as a flap. In performance take a cup with some liquid inside and display the card in the other hand. Make sure you hold the flap against the card so it is not noticeable. Secretly allow the flap to open as you display the cup. Carefully place the cup on top of the card. The extra flap will add more surface area to the card and allow the glass to be balanced on it.

Suggestions:

Take your time when you construct your gimmick. Make sure you set the cup on the edge of the card carefully.

Unbreakable Toothpick

Effect:

Magician displays a handkerchief and a toothpick. The toothpick is set down in the center of the handkerchief. The corners of the handkerchief are closed to cover the toothpick. The toothpick is snapped in half. Everyone in the audience can hear it snap. The magician says the magic word and opens the handkerchief. To the amazement of the audience the toothpick is restored.

Difficulty: medium

Impressiveness: 7

Method:

You have two toothpicks. The audience is only ever aware of one. Take one of the toothpicks and sew it in the hem of the handkerchief. Have your mom help you out with this. This will hide the toothpick in the handkerchief. To perform the trick set the handkerchief on the table. Display a toothpick and place it in the center. Fold over the ends of the handkerchief so the toothpick is covered. Grab the toothpick in the hem. It will look like you are picking up the one you just placed inside. Snap the toothpick in half. Make sure everyone can hear it snap. Say a magic word and open the handkerchief. The toothpick is now restored!

Suggestions:

Take your time when performing this trick. Make sure everyone can hear it snap. Don't open the handkerchief immediately. Build up some suspense as you make the magic happen.

See Illustration:

Sew the toothpick in the hem of the handkerchief.

Instant Freeze

Effect:

The magician pours some water into a cup. The magician snaps his finger and turns the cup upside down. An ice cube falls onto the table. The water has instantly turned into ice!

Difficulty: easy

Impressiveness: 7

Method:

You need to make a gimmick for this trick. I suggest using a mug or an opaque cup. It must be opaque. Take a cheap sponge and cut it so it will fit snugly around the bottom edge of the cup. Use scissors to trim it into shape. The sponge should not be any thicker than about 1.5 inches. Take some glue and glue this into the cup. Let it dry. Your gimmick cup is now complete. Place an ice cube on top of the sponge inside the glass and you are ready to perform. Take a pitcher of water and pour it into the cup. The sponge will soak up the water that you pour in. Don't pour too much in. Just pour enough so that everyone can see that the water is going inside. Tilt the cup from side to side so all the water gets soaked up. This is the time for you to build up suspense. Say a magic word or two and announce that you can instantly freeze water. Now turn the cup upside down and let the ice cube fall onto the table. You have successfully turned water into ice without a freezer!

Suggestions:

You may also make this trick more impromptu. You can use crumpled up napkins in the bottom of the cup. This works well at restaurants. Just make sure no one will see you setting up the trick. Also be sure no one can see inside

the cup. You can practice using different amounts of water.

You will be surprised how much a sponge can soak up.

Ed Junior

Miscellaneous Miracles

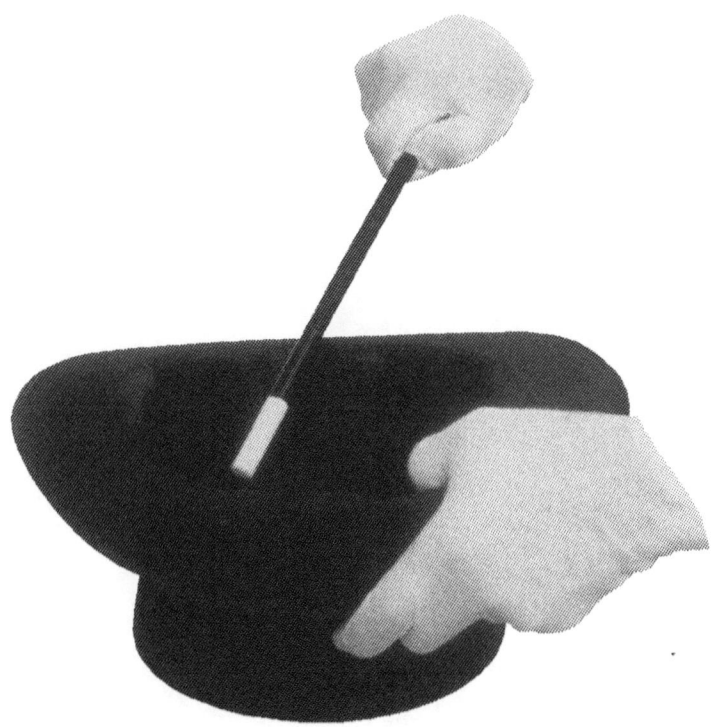

Ed Junior

<u>Miscellaneous Miracles</u>

In this section you will find several other magic tricks that don't fit into a particular category. These tricks will not require any advanced setup. Magic can be performed with almost any object. This section will teach you several unique magic tricks that magicians have been performing for years.

Sometimes on a rainy day I like to go through my older magic books and look at all of the tricks that don't get performed much these days. Magicians are always looking for bigger and newer tricks. The easiest way to perform new magic is by taking an old trick and putting a new twist on it. These are a few tricks I feel should be performed more. I hope you will bring these classics back to life!

Miracle Balloon

Effect:

Magician blows up a balloon. Magically a safety pin is inserted into the balloon but it does not burst!

Difficulty: easy

Impressiveness: 9

Method:

You may of learned this in science class or from a friend. This trick works by secretly applying clear tape to the balloon. Before performing attach a small piece of tape to the balloon. I prefer having the balloon already blown up and then applying the tape. If you don't do this, the tape might fall off while attempting to blow it up. Try it both ways and see what works for you.

Now show the balloon and a safety pin. Slowly insert the pin over top of the tape by piercing the balloon. It will not pop because the tape seals the piercing point. Pull the pin back out and demonstrate that this was only an illusion and then actually pop the balloon.

Suggestions:

You don't have to pop the balloon at the end. Make sure you use clear tape so the audience can't see it on the balloon. Think of some different patter ideas and ways to present this trick for an audience. Example: Mad Scientist, New Product-non-bursting balloons.

Eggstra

Effect:

Magician asks a spectator to pick an egg from a carton. The magician also chooses an egg. They each try and spin the egg. Only the magician can get his egg to spin.

Method:

The spinning egg is hard-boiled, the rest of the eggs are raw. Place one hard-boiled egg in a carton with the rest. Remember where the hard-boiled egg is. Have a spectator choose an egg and try to spin it. They will not succeed. Show them it is possible by spinning yours. In the chance that they accidentally choose the hard-boiled egg, give your spectator a funny look and say, "how did you do that!"

Suggestions:

You could also place the eggs in a bowl. Keeping the hard-boiled egg at a place where only you can reach it. I find it to be more natural by having the eggs in the carton you bought them in.

The Animated Pencil

Effect:

You place a pencil on the table in front of you. Moving your finger forward and at your command the pencil rolls across the table. You hand the pencil to the spectators and they can't duplicate your actions.

Difficulty: easy

Impressiveness: 6

Method:

Many people believe this effect might have something to do with static. The real secret is <u>you carefully blow down on the pencil causing it to roll forward</u>. For this trick you need some misdirection. So I suggest you pretend to rub your finger on your shirt. People will then think that you are using static electricity. After the trick is over hand it to a spectator. They will not be able to do it.

Suggestions:

Make sure you blow straight down on the pencil to get it rolling. Do not blow too much because you might get caught. A little can go a long way.

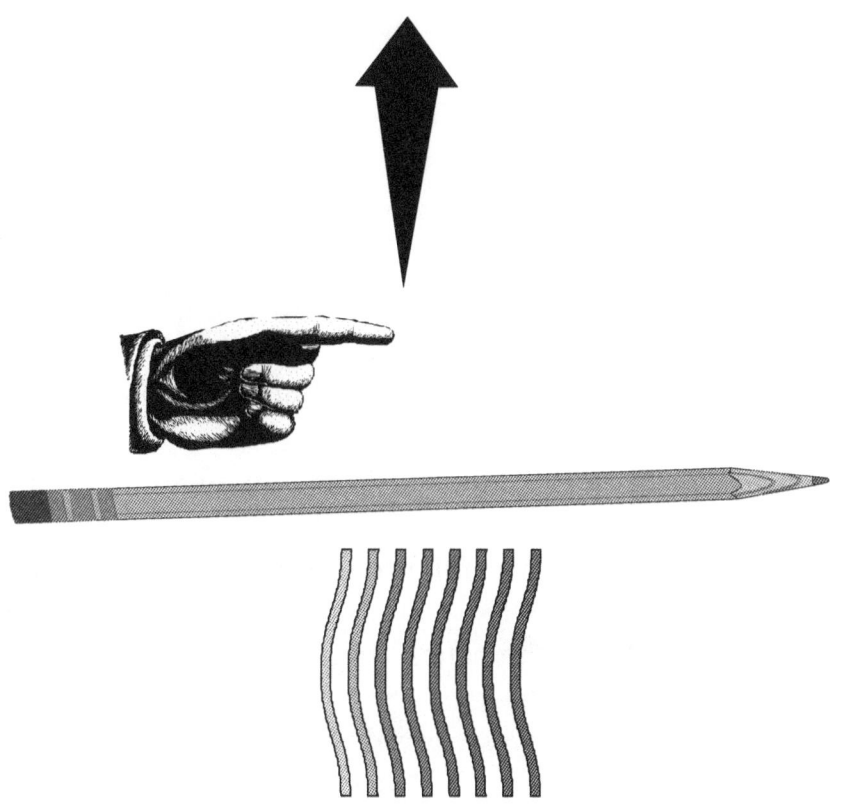

Blow the air secretly from your mouth directly on top of the pencil. This will cause it to slowly roll forward. Draw your finger in front of the pencil as it rolls. It will seem the pencil is following your finger. See Illustration.

<u>Bill Power</u>

Effect:

Magician borrows a dollar bill from a spectator. It is folded in half, lengthwise. A pencil is given to the spectator to hold on to. They are instructed to hold each end firmly so it cannot possibly be dropped. The magician announces that 1-dollar bills have powerful properties. The bill is rested against the middle of the pencil. In a quick motion the bill is brought up and quickly swung down cutting right through the pencil. The pencil has successfully been chopped in half with a borrowed dollar bill!

Difficulty: easy

Impressiveness: 9

Method:

This is easy sleight of hand. When you raise your arm to swing down on the pencil your index finger is placed along side the dollar bill. Your finger smashes down through the pencil easily. After you see the pencil chopped in half quickly pull your index finger back so no one will see. This is a powerful, yet very easy magic stunt to perform.

Suggestions:

Use an unsharpened pencil. Make sure the spectator firmly holds the pencil. Carry a few pencils and a dollar in your pocket and your ready to go.

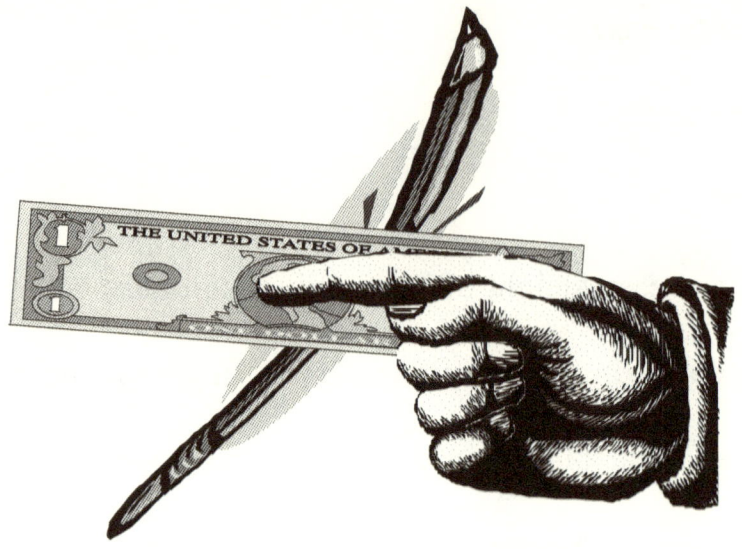

Magnetic Silverware

Effect:

Magician places a spoon in his left fist. The right hand squeezes his wrist. The magician opens his finger and the spoon seems to be clinging with no means of support.

Difficulty: easy

Impressiveness: 6

Method:

Have the spoon placed in your left hand by making a fist to hold it. Your right hand grabs your left wrist. Secretly you slip your index finger inside your fist. Firmly press the spoon against your palm. Open your fingers of the left hand and the spoon looks to be clinging to your hand. To finish the trick release your finger pressure and allow the spoon to fall onto the table.

Suggestions:

Only perform this stunt for a few seconds. If you hold it too long the spectators might start staring at your hand. The more they have a chance to stare, the better of a chance they might figure it out. This is a good quick magic stunt to do in a restaurant. Try using other objects for example: A magic wand, pencil, fork, etc.

It Bounces!

Effect:

The magician seated at a table takes a dinner roll and claims that he can bounce it off the floor. He throws it downward and immediately everyone sees it fly five feet in the air.

Difficulty: medium

Impressiveness: 8

Method:

This trick is totally impromptu. The only requirement is that you need to be seated at a table. When you take the roll you only pretend to toss it downward. When you do this, make a tapping noise with your foot. Immediately after you tap your foot; flick your wrist up so that it tosses the roll into the air. The audience never sees the roll bounce but they assume it has because of the noise heard and they see it fly in the air.

Suggestions:

Timing is the most important factor in this trick. Fake tossing the roll, tapping your foot and flicking your wrist should all happen simultaneously.

Make sure your hand is not seen tossing up the roll. Keep it below table and eye level. Try using other objects that people think you can't bounce. Try some of these:

- Deck of cards
- Fruit (apple, orange, pear, etc.)
- Vegetables (Broccoli, Turnip, etc.)
- Cups (use plastic)

Linking Paper Clips

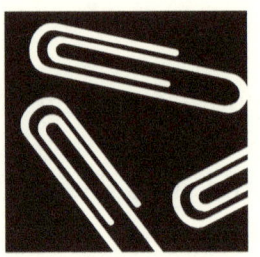

Effect:

A dollar bill is shown along with two paper clips. The bill is accordion folded and each paper clip is attached holding the separate sides together. The magician snap his fingers and than pull sharply on the bill in opposite directions. The two paper clips fly off the bill and are actually linked together.

Difficulty: easy

Impressiveness: 6

Method:

Borrow a dollar bill. Fold it like an accordion or in a "Z" type pattern. Attach each paper clip to opposite sides of the bill. One clip is attached to first and second folds and the

other clip is attached to the second and third folds. When setup properly all you have to do is grip both ends of the bill and pull them apart. This snaps the paper clips in the air and they seemingly link in mid air.

Suggestions:

When pulling the bill apart you can do it slow or fast. It is amazing either way!

Ed Junior

Illusions

Ed Junior

<u>Illusions</u>

Illusions are big time magic. An illusion is a large trick involving a person/persons or a large object. I have selected two illusions that can be performed impromptu. These illusions require no special props; all you need to perform them is yourself! I suggest practicing these tricks many times just like all the other tricks you wish to learn. These illusions are best performed only after you prove to your audience that you are good at what you do. If you are asked to perform them more than once, don't!

Before I get into discussing how to float yourself and twist your arm impossibly I wanted to give you a list of the magic worlds most famous illusions. Many of these illusions are hundreds of years old but yet they easily thrill any crowd today.

The 10 Most Famous Illusions

1. Sawing in Half

2. Metamorphosis

3. Zigzag Girl

4. Levitation of a Woman

5. Water Torture Cell

6. Guillotine

7. Sword Suspension

8. Floating Ball

9. Appearing or Vanishing Elephant

10. Sword Box

The Ultimate Self-Floatation

Effect:

You ask a few spectators to stand behind you and you instruct them to catch you in case you happen to fall. With your back to them you start floating a few inches off the ground! You float back down and walk away.

Difficulty: hard

Impressiveness: 10

Method:

This trick is more than worth the price of this book. I include it here because it is fun, easy to do, and very baffling. This is true impromptu magic. You can do it anytime, and almost anywhere. There is nothing to purchase, or build. How do you float? This is a true magic illusion. You stand on the toes of your left foot keeping yourself balanced while your right foot rises a few inches off the ground. Keep your feet together when performing the floatation. Have your audience stand behind you about 3-5 feet so that they are watching you from the back. Have them angled at five o'clock. This means they should only be able to see your right shoe and the back of your left shoe. When you start to float, rise up slowly and hold your arms out perpendicular to the ground. It will look like you are pushing yourself off the ground with your arms. Float for a few seconds and than drop back down onto both feet. This trick requires that you only perform it for 1-3 people.

If you perform for too many some of them will see you standing on one foot.

This illusion also requires excellent patter and audience buildup. I suggest you perform a few tricks and then float for them.

Suggestions:

Only use this effect every so often. Don't ruin it by performing it all the time. Save it for the proper time. A good idea is too build up the suspense and interest in what you are about to do. Many people after seeing you float will say you floated much higher than you really did. Make sure you are wearing pants for the illusion. The pants help cover your feet from between your legs.

Double Jointed

Effect:

You stick your arms out in front of you, and you ask the audience to mimic what you do. You turn both hands palm out, leaving both of your thumbs pointing down to the ground. Your left hand is placed over the right and your fingers are all locked together. On the count of three the magician twists his arms back up so his hands are now untwisted and back to normal. Everyone in the audience still has their arms twisted in all different directions.

Method:

This magic effect relies all on misdirection. Have the audience follow your steps. Place your arms out in front. Palm outward and thumbs towards the floor. Place your left hand over the right and lock all your fingers together. You mention again to the audience to keep their thumbs pointed down. When you say this bring your hands briefly apart and motion with your thumbs that they need to keep their thumbs pointed down. Bring your hands back together but give your right arm a full twist to the right. Place your left hand back on top and lock your fingers together. Your hands will look exactly the same as the spectators. Tell them on your cue to give their arms a twist and to right themselves. You will be able too and no one in the audience will.

Suggestions:

I suggest that you do not perform this as your first trick. Also when performing this stunt please do not give them any indication as to what the outcome will be. Telling someone what the trick is might allow someone to figure out the secret. Make sure everyone is participating with this illusion! I suggest this can be the first trick you perform in your routine. This gets their attention and catches them all off guard.

Ed Junior

Ed Junior

<u>Impromptu</u>

<u>Puzzles And</u>

<u>Games</u>

Impromptu Puzzles and Games

This section covers puzzles and games that you can perform almost anywhere. I include puzzles in this book for an important reason. When entertaining an audience you do not have to perform many tricks. If you perform one or two tricks and perform some puzzles it really will add entertainment value to your performance. Tricks can sometimes seem repetitive to an audience. Being able to add something different such as a puzzle or two will keep them entertained.

It is important that you do not perform every trick you know to an audience all at one time. If the same audience sees you again you will not have anything new to perform and you definitely do not want to repeat a trick. Give them a taste of what you can do and save the rest of your tricks for a later time.

I'd Like To Buy A Vowel

Description: The magician announces that he can say up to one hundred different words without using the letter "A" in any of them. No one believes this. With every bodies attention the magician proceeds to say one hundred completely different words without using the letter "A"!

Can you figure this puzzle out?

Method:

To do this, announce to everyone that you will say one hundred different words without using the letter "A". Believe me, no one will take you seriously. Make sure to have the attention of everyone. To achieve the feat simply start counting. Example: one, two, three, four, five, six, seven, eight, nine, ten, eleven... and so on. You simply count out loud from 1-100.

Suggestion:

You could also say 1000 words without using the letter "A". Count from 0-999. One thousand is the first word using the letter "A". Make sure you say each number without adding the word "and" to it. For example: "one hundred <u>and</u> one" You may also choose to start at the number zero. It is very amazing; remember that you achieve this because none of the numbers 1-10 have the letter "A" in the spelling.

<u>Easy Addition?</u>

Description:

The magician announces to all that 11+3=2 or 9+6=3. Everyone looks at the magician in confusion. He says this formula is true anywhere in the world.

Is this true or is it a bold lie?

Method:

This puzzle is true. Many people think you are talking about straight addition. In a way you are. Take a look at a clock or a watch. If it is 11 o'clock and you add three hours it becomes 2 o'clock. If it is 9 o'clock and you add six hours that equals 3 o'clock. Pretty tricky eh?

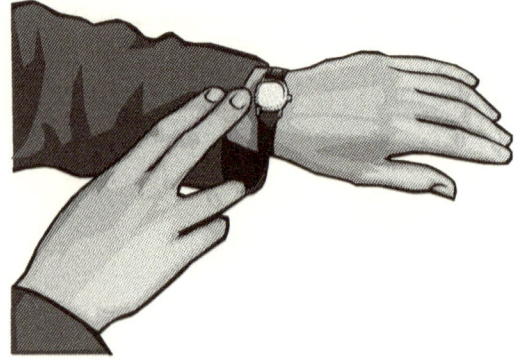

A few fun and entertaining questions to ask your audience

1. How many animals of each did Moses have on the arc?

2. Say silk five times fast. Silk, silk, silk, silk, silk.
   What do cows drink?

3. Why can't a man living in Pennsylvania be buried
   west of the Mississippi?

Audience Responses: (your audience will usually say
this)

1. 2 of each animal

2. Water

3. For this one either your audience knows or they
   don't!

Real Answers:

1. Moses did not have an arc, Noah did.

2. Cows drink water, they give milk.

3. The man is alive

Pennies For Your Thoughts

Description:

Nine pennies are displayed and laid into two rows. One row has four pennies and the other row has five. Can you move just one penny so both rows will have a total of five coins each?

Try and figure this puzzle out. Take nine pennies and follow the directions. You cannot add extra pennies. You may only move one penny and both rows must contain five pennies.

Method:

Lay out the pennies as described earlier. Take the extra penny in the row of five and stack it on top of the penny that connects each row. You now have five pennies in two rows. Even though it is stacked on top you really still have

five pennies in each row.

See the illustration.

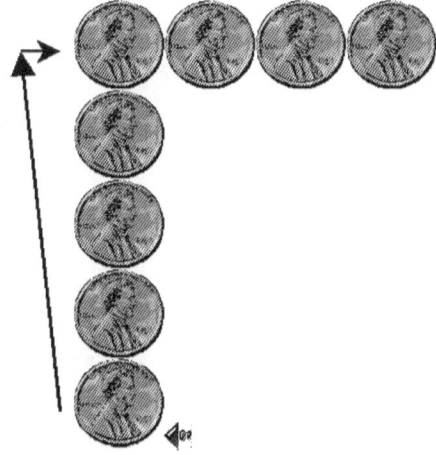

Stack the penny at the first arrow on top of the other penny.

Follow the arrows.

Multi Color Pencil

Description:

You announce to the audience that it is possible to write more than one color with a regular number two pencil. You prove this by shading in different colors of gray on a piece of paper. You then announce it is possible to write any color that someone names.

Is this possible to do with a regular pencil?

Method:

It is possible. You need to make sure you word this puzzle properly to your audience. Tell your audience you will attempt to write any color named on a piece of paper with a led pencil. Ask someone to name any color. They will not believe you but now it's your chance to prove them wrong. When they announce the color, for example blue, write the word <u>blue</u> on the piece of paper. You have successfully written a chosen color with a regular pencil. After you perform this you will get moans and groans.

Suggestions:

The audience in this puzzle gets the wool pulled over their eyes. They assume that you will write with different colors from the pencil. In this puzzle the word **write** is a key word. You do write blue but not the way they assumed. Have fun with this one!

This is what your piece of paper should look like when performing the puzzle.

Balanced

Description:

You ask a spectator to balance a penny on the edge of a dollar bill. He/she tries and fails. The magician demonstrates his skill and amazingly balances a penny on the edge of the dollar bill. Give it a try yourself. Is this actually possible?

Difficulty: medium

Impressiveness: 8

Method:

This puzzle takes a bit of skill and very steady hands but it is possible to do. Take a dollar bill and make a very sharp crease in its center by folding in half. Use your fingernails to make the crease as sharp as you can. Set the bill down on the table by sitting it on its edge. Carefully place a penny in the center of the bill where you made the crease. It will balance on there. To finish this puzzle, grab the sides of the bill with your hands. Lift the bill up slowly about 1-2 inches off the table. As you do this pull the bill taught. The penny will remain balanced on top!

Suggestions:

This puzzle requires a good deal of practice. When picking the bill up do it slowly and smoothly. Do not lift the bill up too high because the penny will fall off. The penny balances because of the crease you put in the bill. It gives the penny more of a surface area to rest on. When you pull the bill taught the crease still remains but it is very hard to see. Enjoy this one!

See Illustration:

<u>The line in the middle of the bill represents the crease.</u>

<u>Stop Egging Me On!</u>

Description:

Two shot glasses are set on the table one aside of the other. An egg is placed in one glass. Is it possible to get the egg into the other glass without touching it in any way? You can't use your hands and you can't use any other item. Is it possible? See if you can figure this one out.

Ed Junior

Difficulty: medium

Impressiveness: 9

Method:

This puzzle is one of my favorites. All you need is two small shot glasses and an egg. Set the glasses so that they are right next to each other. Place an egg in one of the glasses. The trick to this puzzle is to use your mouth. If you blow air angled towards the bottom of the egg it will lift it out of the glass and it will land in the other. This sounds easy but you have to blow in the right place. A quick short wind should be enough to make it work. The air pressure builds up in the glass and pops the egg out. Don't get yourself dizzy over this one!

Suggestions:

Have a spectator figure out the puzzle. If he says that it is not possible you can now prove him wrong.

See Illustration:

Blow air directly down on egg. See arrow.

Toothpick Maniac

Description:

Ask a spectator to take nine toothpicks and make ten. They will look at you in a very confused manner. Is it possible to make ten from nine toothpicks?

Difficulty: easy

Impressiveness: 5

Method:

Once you see how this works you are going to laugh at how easy it is. Take the nine toothpicks and spell ten.

Suggestions:

You can use matches instead of toothpicks. When you ask the spectator to take nine toothpicks and make ten they will be very confused. It will seem impossible to do. After you perform this puzzle accept the moans and groans as

applause. They shouldn't be too harsh on you.

See Illustration:

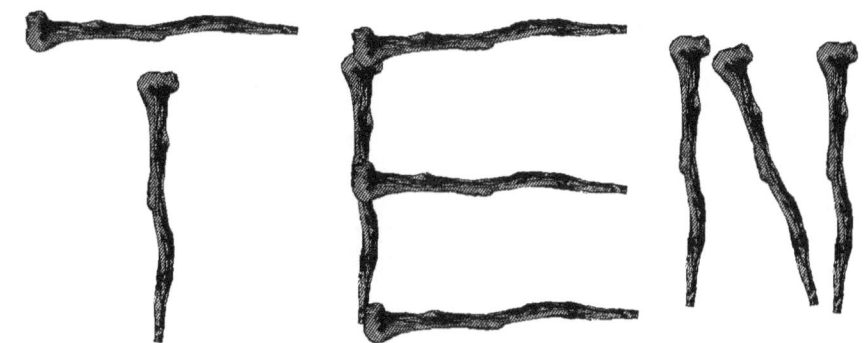

Ed Junior

Magic Organizations

There are many magic organizations worldwide that have thousands of members. Feel free to visit their websites and ask for more information. Through organizations like these magicians can learn from one another, share secrets, compete against one another for awards and teach one another through educational lectures on different magic topics. Even the most famous magicians of today are members of these organizations. The reason is because there is truly something for everyone. There are so many benefits you can receive by becoming a member. Take a look at some of the larger magic organizations.

- The Society of American Magicians
  P.O. Box 510260
  St. Louis, MO 61351
  (314) 846-5659
  www.ueletric.com/sam
  rmblowers@aol.com

- The International Brotherhood of Magicians
  11137-C South Town Square
  St. Louis, MO 63123-7819
  (314) 845-9200
  www.magician.org
  No1inMagic@aol.com

Closing Remarks

I hope this magical journey was as much fun for you as it has been for me. Magic is one of the greatest art forms ever. Magic has no boundaries; anyone can learn it secrets and become a magician. I urge you to continue learning magic by visiting magic shops, reading books and watching magic shows on television. Review the magic in this book, practice it, perform it and enjoy the magic, as it is now a part of your life. I hope you learned that the most important thing is not the trick itself but rather how it is performed, for it is you that will create the real magic.

Magically Yours,

Ed Junior

Contact Information For Ed Junior:
(610) 775-2493
www.edjunior.com
freereport@edjunior.com
Creating Unforgettable Events And Parties For You, Guaranteed!

Ed Junior

<u>Time For A Party</u>

(Parents, Learn How To Easily Create An Unforgettable Party For Your Child, Guaranteed!)

The easiest way to get the most out of this guide is to read through it entirely first. Then read it again making notes on things you like and any other ideas you may come up with. This way you can look at your notes, and start planning that birthday party!

A child's birthday party can be the most exciting experience for your child. Make sure you follow all of the steps thoroughly and give yourself enough planning time. This guide will prevent you from any party disasters!

Planning The Party:

As I said before, make sure you leave yourself enough time to plan your party. The worst situation to be in is waiting until the last minute. <u>You should start planning your party at least 4 weeks in advance</u>. This will give you enough time to buy supplies and food, create a guest list, and hire entertainment. **A very helpful idea is to have a back up plan** just in case something goes wrong. For example, if your planning a party outside, and bad weather occurs, a good back up plan would be to have extra games and events inside your house all ready to go.

How Long Should The Party Be?

In my experiences parties should last no longer than 2 hours. In these 2 hours you will have plenty of time for entertainment, games, meals, and gifts. If your party is too long, the children might become bored, and even disruptive. Remember children have short attention spans and can get bored quickly, so don't overdue it. If you're going to send invitations, make sure you specify what time the party will begin. This makes sure everyone arrives in time and doesn't miss anything!

How Many Should We Invite?

The average child's party consists of 8-15 children and 5-10 adults. I realize your child may plead to you to invite all of his or her friends. Don't give in. Most people truly only have between 5-10 true friends. These are friends that your child plays with, and spends time with the most. These are the children you should invite. If too many children are invited this increases the chance of an argument or scuffle. Again, the easiest way to avoid these problems is too only invite close friends, and close family. Sit down with your child and make a list of possible people to invite. Keep it limited. The list should include full names and phone numbers.

What To Do When Your Child Says, "My friend is also having a party on that day, Mommy!"

The best way to avoid this situation is to plan your party around other parties, sporting events, and other family activities. This is the case for your own family, and the families of your guests. This will also insure that the people you decide to invite are available and able to attend. Remember, all of this should be discussed before sending out party invitations.

The Best Place To Have The Party

Truly, the best environment for your child is the home environment. You could have the party in a restaurant, bowling ally, Chuckie Cheese, or other venues. Some of these places have reasonable packages and rates; however, children tend to get out of control, and run around doing whatever they want. In some cases it is even hard to get the kids to sit down and eat because there are so many other things to do. The best place to have the party is at home. This puts everyone at ease, including you and your child. Having control of the environment that the party is held in is the key to a successful party.

Food Time!!!!

The easiest way to save money when planning a party is to not provide a complete meal for your party guests. The way to do this is easy. Plan your party around meal times, such as 2pm-4pm. This time is perfect because every single guest should have had some sort of breakfast and lunch before they arrive at your party. If they do get hungry they only have to wait until 4pm to leave and get dinner. Of course you will still be serving snacks and drinks. This should easily hold over any empty stomachs. If you plan a party at or near a mealtime such as 12 noon or 5 pm you can inexpensively provide tasty food. Here are some suggestions for snacks and meals.

- Baby vegetables, and fruit

- Pretzels, or chips

- Small Pizza

- Cereal bars

- Crackers

- Dip

- Pizza (bake your own, or order for delivery)

- Hot dogs/ Hamburgers

- Sandwiches

I would suggest that you choose only a few of these items for your party. If you have too many choices the children might start complaining and want to change their mind on what they are hungry for. This also keeps down the chances of any large food fights! These foods are all easy to maintain and prepare. Have fun, and happy eating!

"Wow, Am I Parched!"

As with the food, drinks are no different. Don't choose too many different kinds of liquids to drink, keep it simple! Here is a list of some liquids the children will like...

- Water

- Lemonade

- Hawaiian Punch

- Coke or Sprite

- Juice Boxes

- Milk (the children might request it, especially for the cake!)

I really think the juice boxes are terrific. They don't cost very much, you can get many different varieties, and you don't need a cup! A helpful hint: Make sure not to serve the children too much to drink or eat at first. They need room for cake and dessert! If you do serve too much to drink you will have a line of children ready to go to the bathroom!

Time For CAKE!!!!

The easiest and most inexpensive option is to bake the cake yourself on your own! If you don't like baking, ask a friend or relative. Another idea is to serve cupcakes instead! They are easy to bake, come in many good flavors, and are the perfect size for children to eat. Place all of the cupcakes on a pretty serving tray and place the appropriate number of candles in them.

Time For DESSERT!!! Burp!

I suggest you don't overdue the junk foods, but hey it is your child's party! A good and easy dessert is ice cream. Search around different supermarkets and dairies to find those small ice cream cups. They usually come with a wooden spoon. They also come in the 3 most popular flavors, chocolate, vanilla, and strawberry. A helpful hint: Buy some berries, whipped topping, and chocolate syrup for those wild children!

We Need Supplies!!!

Party stores are fine for finding what you need. However, I suggest the dollar store. There has been a huge boom in these stores and they are very popular. Why? You can find stuff you need, cheap. You will find all of your needs there… Such as:

Party Invitations

Balloons

Streamers

Party Favors

Gift Wrap, Bags

Paper Cups

Paper Plates

Paper Napkins

Plastic Utensils

You can easily create small party bags to hand out to each child who attends the party. This gives the children some extra pleasure for coming.

Bits of Business...

This section covers stuff you might not even have thought about. It is a good idea to put some sort of decorations outside of your house so anyone who will be attending can easily find your home. Just in case, have a First Aid Kit handy. As guests arrive take the presents and place them in a separate room. When children see presents they get very excited and want to open them at the wrong time. Keep them out of reach, and out of sight. A great idea to add some atmosphere to your party is to play some background music. Pick something the kids will enjoy. You could even hold a small dance contest and hand out prizes to every child who participates. Another great idea for the party and for backup situations is to have a few movies on hand. Here is a brief list:

Classic Movies

Comedy Movies

Cartoons

Other fun ideas to pass by time:

- Karaoke

- Card Games

- Mini Carnival

- Mini Casino Party (use candy or party favors as winnings)

- Door Prizes

- Costume Contest (have a box of clothing that you don't' need and let the children come up with fun ideas)

- Mini Game Show

Make sure all the movies you select will interest the children and will be appropriate for their age. If you are planning a movie time for the party I would suggest placing it near the end of your party. Movies tend to make children tired and this is perfect for when the party is just about to end.

Many parents will not stay for the party. They will drop their children off and come back later to pick them up. Make sure the parents know when to pick them up. Otherwise the party might end and you're stuck with a home full of children!

A List Of Great Companies For Your Party Needs!!!!

- US Toy-www.ustoy.com

- Rhode Island Novelty www.rinco.com

- Oriental Trading www.Orientaltrading.com

I highly recommend these companies. You can find party supplies, games, carnival games, gifts, prizes, favors, decorations, and more. Please note some of them do have a minimum order amount. You can also request a free catalog.

Secrets To Maintain Your Budget:

Make your own invitations on your computer. There are many great programs that provide you with ready-made designs, or you could create your own from scratch.

Another way to save money is to plan your party around meal times. This will save you from having to provide an entire meal. You still need to serve drinks and snacks!

DON'T overdue the party decorations. Remember, these will only last the day of the party. If you have too many decorations some children might start tearing them down for something fun to do. You certainly do not want that, and it would be a waste of money.

The optimal situation is running out of snack foods. Please be sure you have enough cake and dessert. The children cherish the birthday dessert the most. Snack foods are only there to hold everyone over until mealtime, or cake/desert time. So if you run out, it's ok!

We Need Entertainment!

I placed this last in the party guide, as it is the most expensive investment to make. Hiring entertainment can really make or break the party. If you feel you have enough activities, games, and movies to keep all the children happy for 2 hours than congrats! If not, here are some very important secrets I will share with you.

Magicians, Clowns, Face Painters, Puppeteers

Out of all of these, the magician is really the most popular birthday entertainer. A professional magician should offer you different types of party packages, containing different program lengths and extras. Any good entertainer should offer goodie bags in their package. I urge you to call around to see what kind of great party entertainment packages you can find. Most magicians can offer you a 30-40 minute show in the price range between $75.00-$100.00.

A professional entertainer should provide you with needed information such as testimonials, business cards, resume, etc. If this entertainer you speak to does not meet this criteria, I suggest talking to another.

You should also ask for a performance agreement/contract from the entertainer you decide to hire. This insures you, and them that everything is set. Party times, dates, contact info and pricing should all be included on the agreement.

A Quick Review Of Important Information You Need To Know Before Hiring Any Entertainer

1. Make sure the entertainer is professional in every aspect not just including the show. This means he/she should be able to provide you with needed references and a performance agreement.

2. Paying the lowest price for an entertainer is not always the best idea. You get what you pay for; low prices = low quality entertainment. Pay a little extra and you will be more than satisfied with your choice. Hire someone who entertains full time. A full time entertainer has to be good if they perform for a living.

3. Every entertainer should provide you with a choice of entertainment packages. It is always

good to have choices. You will get more for your money this way.

4. Make sure the entertainer has give away items or handouts. If not, you can create party bags yourself very inexpensively. An entertainer who offers party bags will make your job much easier.

5. The entertainer you hire should offer you a guarantee. Most entertainers don't, so if they give you lousy service your stuck with it.

6. Any entertainer that guarantees his/her performance is a quality entertainer, guaranteed.

Leave Room For The Entertainer

Make sure if you hire an entertainer that you have room for him to perform. Professional entertainers should not require much room, but it really helps both of you out. Keep the children away from the entertainer until the show is to begin. Many children get anxious, and really excited. The entertainer might not be able to set up properly if he/she is being bothered. So, keep the children busy!

Investment Overview

- Party Supplies $45.00

- Food, Cake/dessert $ 50.00

- Entertainment $100.00

- Total Party Investment. $195.00

This total investment will vary in different parts of the country. Again, your entertainment investment is the highest. <u>The key is to spend less on party supplies</u>. This will allow you to have extra food and entertainment money.

Don't Forget!

- Camera

- Film

- Video Camera (if available)

This party will leave your entire family with lasting memories. Make sure you capture them on film. You can buy very inexpensive throwaway cameras. The cameras take good quality pictures and are easy to use. Make sure you use all your film because it will be worth it!

To Do List

Here is stuff to do at least 4 weeks before your party...

- Make a guest list, complete with names and numbers.

- Decide where your party will take place. Away from your home? Inside, or Outside? Beware of the weather!

- Decide on the food menu

- Hire an entertainer

- Decide on Games/Activities

- Decide on the time and date of party

Stuff to do about 2 weeks before the party

- Send out invitations or call and invite (use your guest list)

- Create or purchase party supplies and decorations. (dollar store)

- Make an extra grocery list of essentials (garbage bags, snack foods)

Stuff to do one week before the party

- Confirm entertainment

- Purchase groceries (items that won't spoil)

- Check to see if invitations were received (see who is coming)

Stuff to do a few days before the party

- Call guests on list to remind them about your party

- Bake the cake/cupcakes (have friend/relative help)

- Get grill working if needed for hotdogs/hamburgers

- Clean house (make child friendly)

- Get film for camera and batteries

- Purchase other food items (finishing purchasing items on grocery list)

The day before your party

- Prepare any food or snack trays etc.

- Review party schedule and any list minute business

- Make your home child friendly (clean, put away papers, money, expensive items)

- Start to decorate

<u>The day of the party</u>

- Prepare any other food items

- Finish decorating

- Setup games

- Setup snacks, prepare table

- Relax before your guests arrive!!!

<u>NOTES</u>

<u>NOTES</u>

<u>NOTES</u>

<u>NOTES</u>

ABOUT THE AUTHOR

Ed Junior has been interested in magic since the age of five. The first magic trick he learned was a gift from his uncle Alan Kappenstein. His interest in magic continued to expand over the years. Ed spent all of his allowance money on magic books and tricks. From these simple magic books and tricks Ed has taken a fascinating hobby and molded it into a full time profession. He performs all types of shows ranging from private parties to stage shows in Las Vegas, Nevada. Ed also teaches magic to thousands of people every year at the Mingus Magic Shop in Reading, Pennsylvania. Ed Junior is twenty-two years old and resides in Mohnton, Pennsylvania.